GRACE WORDS FROM THE CROSS

Messages For Lent,
Holy Week Or Good Friday

BY JOHN R. BROKHOFF

C.S.S Publishing Co., Inc.
Lima, Ohio

GRACE WORDS FROM THE CROSS

Copyright © 1992 by
The C.S.S. Publishing Company, Inc.
Lima, Ohio

Reprinted 1993
Reprinted 1994

Scripture quotations are from the New Revised Standard Version of the Bible, copyright 1989 by the Division of Christian Education of the National Council of the Churches of Christ in the USA. Used by permission.

9200 / ISBN 1-55673-382-8   PRINTED IN U.S.A.

Father, forgive them; for they know not what they are doing.

— Luke 23:34

God Kisses The World

Introduction

Have you ever put an "X" or two beside your name when you signed a valentine or a love letter? This was your way of sending kisses of love.

Did you ever wonder why an "X" stood for a kiss? The origin of using an "X" for a kiss goes back to ancient times when some were unable to write their names on important documents. In place of the name, an "X" was used. To prove one's sincerity in keeping the contract, the person then placed a kiss on the "X." Even in our day when we are asked to sign a paper, the person in charge indicates the place for our signature with an "X."

The cross is God's "X." By the cross God kisses the world to show his love for sinners and to guarantee his faithfulness to his promises. The "X" is a form of the cross. It is known as St. Andrew's cross, for, according to tradition, he was martyred on a cross of that shape. By the cross God is sending us his love. "God so loved the world that he gave his only Son." In a Lenten hymn, Charles Wesley has us sing, "O Love Divine, What Hast Thou Done?" He closes each stanza, "My Lord, my love, is crucified."

This love of God is greater than all other loves. It is an agape love, one that is not deserved. A better word for it is grace. During the three hours Jesus was on the cross, from noon until three, Jesus gave seven words of grace. Upon these words of grace we will meditate, one by one. May the meditations of our hearts be acceptable to you, O Redeemer!

Possible Uses Of The Book

This book deals with the Lenten-Holy Week season. It can be used in several ways:

1. For personal, individual meditation and reflection to strengthen faith and to develop a deeper appreciation of the cross.

2. For a series of messages during Lent: one Word for each of the six weeks of Lent and the seventh Word for Holy Week.

3. For a series of sermons for each day of Holy Week.

4. For meditations during the Good Friday three-hour service, noon to 3 p.m.

A Grace Word Of Mercy

The First Word

Father, forgive them; for they know not what they are doing."   *— Luke 23:34*

Jesus' first word of love deals with his enemies. He prayed, "Father, forgive them; for they know not what they are doing." This prayer expresses amazing grace. He is asking his Father to forgive those who unjustly accused him of blasphemy, who whipped and mocked him, who ridiculed him with a crown of thorns, who drove big nails into his hands and feet. They tortured and murdered him in the cruelest way possible. The scene is like an active volcano which is steaming and bubbling up from the fiery depth below. The hatred, jealousy and bigotry were red hot, and here Jesus responds with the cool beauty of love's forgiveness. In spite of this, Jesus asks God to forgive them. How can this be? Only a God could do something like that! Not only does Jesus ask for their pardon but he even gives God a reason for forgiving them. He actually makes excuses for his murderers! Can you believe it? His

9

reason is, "They know not what they are doing." What did his enemies not know? Do we, too, sin because we do not know what we are doing?

Sin Is Against God

Jesus prayed, "Father, forgive . . ." Why should the Father forgive? Why doesn't Jesus forgive those wicked people? After all, he was the one suffering and dying. God the Father was in heaven, was he not?

Apparently Jesus' enemies did not know that all sin is against God. The sin we commit against our fellow humans is at the same time committed against God. Seven of the Ten Commandments deal with our duties to fellow human beings.

Consider the sin of David. He committed adultery with Bathsheba and had her husband murdered so that he could marry her and cover up the fact of their illegitimate son. When his sin was called to his attention by Nathan, the prophet, David confessed, "I have sinned against the Lord." He did not say he sinned against Bathsheba nor Uriah nor his other wives. It was a sin against God.

Consider another case. When the Prodigal Son came to his senses and decided to return home, he humbly confessed to his father, "I have sinned against heaven . . ." By "heaven" he meant God. He did not consider his sin to be against his brother or mother. It was God who was disobeyed when he ran away from home.

So it was with Jesus' enemies. In their pride and bigotry they thought they were doing a good thing by getting rid of one they considered a lawbreaker. If they had just known they were sinning against God, the passion of Christ might never have happened.

And is it not true with us also? Do we think we are sinning against God when we break the laws of the state, when we kill, steal, lie, cheat and commit adultery? Every wrong doing, every unkind word is a sin against God who holds us accountable. When a crime is committed, it is not only the breaking of the state's laws but also the laws of God. Consider the case of a college student who killed her illegitimate son in the college dorm commode. While she may be acquitted by a jury, she still faces the judgment of God. When a man murders his mother, wife and three children, he may get away with it, as he did for 17 years, but he can never get away with it with God. Maybe if people would realize that the harm they do is not only against the state or fellow humans but also against God, it would be at lease one solution to crime. The next time we are tempted to sin we need to remember that yielding is sin against God. To him we are ultimately accountable and face his judgment.

Sin Crucifies Christ

"They know not what they do." Did they not know who that man was on the cross? Jesus prayed, "Forgive them," not "Forgive me." Jesus had no sin to confess. He did not have to ask for forgiveness. He was the sinless, the perfect one. He once challenged his enemies, "Which of you convinceth me of sin?" In a recent church periodical an author accused Jesus of stealing. He wrote: "It's Palm Sunday, so I want you to go into town and steal me a donkey. If anyone catches you, tell them I need it." Even the suggestion that Jesus stole is blasphemous! Jesus' enemies did not know they were killing God's only Son, the sinless one. They were putting to death the very one who came to save them from death.

Horrors! They were crucifying God, for as Paul said, "God was in Christ reconciling the world to himself." No wonder we tremble, tremble when we see Jesus, the very Son of God, in the agony of death. The truth is that by our sins we are still crucifying God's Son. On the Damascus road Jesus asked Paul, "Saul, Saul, why do you persecute me?" How was he re-crucifying Christ? By his persecution of Christian people!

11

Your sins and mine keep Christ on the cross. Each sin is a hammer blow driving nails into his precious hands and feet. The nails we use are the nails of pride, hatred, selfishness and greed. Edward Arlington Robinson reminds us of this in his poem:

Friendliness and faint, with martyred steps and slow,
Faint for the flesh, but for the spirit free,
Stung by the mob that came to see the show,
The Master toiled along to Calvary:
We gibed him as he went, with houndish glee,
Till his dim eyes for us did overflow:
We cursed his vengeless hands thrice wretchedly, —
And this was nineteen hundred years ago.

But after nineteen hundred years the shame
Still clings, and we have not made good the loss
That outraged faith has entered into his name.
Ah, when shall come love's courage to be strong!
Tell me, O Lord — tell me, O Lord, how long
Are we to keep Christ writhing on the cross?

Sin Damages

They did not know what they were doing when they put Jesus on the cross. In their bigotry and self-righteousness they had no idea the harm they were doing not only to Jesus but to many others. Did they realize how much pain they were causing innocent people? Consider the remorse to Jesus' family they caused. What about the despair and fear caused in the disciples? What about the tears shed over their obstinacy in not accepting him? And consider what their treatment of Jesus meant to God the Father. It broke his heart. In an old Roman Catholic cathedral in Savannah, Georgia, a few years ago I saw on the chancel wall a symbol of a red heart in which was a cross. But the heart was broken. Jesus' enemies did not know they were breaking the very heart of God.

12

If only we knew what hurt, pain and heartbreak our sins cause God and people, we would think twice before sinning. A young man driving his car under the influence of alcohol caused an accident in which a girl was crippled for life. A wise judge did not send him to jail, but to serve six months in a hospital emergency room where he could see what damage is done to people by auto accidents and drunken drivers: broken bones, disfigured faces, a life in a wheelchair. When you see the consequences of sin, you hate sin with a passion.

When Jesus prayed to his Father to forgive, he also forgave his killers. If we claim the name of Jesus and consider ourselves to be the people of God, should we also forgive those who hurt us? It may be the most difficult thing we are ever called upon to do. During the Second World War a little girl of Belgium went into her bombed-out church to pray. The roof had fallen in, walls were damaged, stained glass was scattered on the floor and the altar was split in two. She knelt before the altar to pray the Lord's Prayer. She got along well until she came to "as we forgive." How could she forgive the Nazis who destroyed the church and bombed her city and killed some of her friends? She tried and tried but could not make herself say the words. She tried once more and when she got to that place, a gentle voice behind her said, "As we forgive those who trespass against us" and completed the prayer. She turned to see who it was and found it was the king of Belgium. We have the King of kings behind us today and he helps us say, "As we forgive."

A Grace Word Of Promise

The Second Word

"Today you will be with me in paradise.
— *Luke 23:43*

As you have traveled by car around the country, have you noticed from time to time three crosses close to the highway? As an expression of gratitude to God a man in recent years at his own expense has been erecting three crosses. This second word, a grace word of promise, from the cross reminds us that there were not one but three crosses: one for Jesus and the other two for criminals sentenced to die for their misdeeds.

To one of the thieves Jesus gives a loving word or promise: "Today you will be with me in paradise." Here is a case when grace seems ridiculous and unreasonable. He promises heaven to one who has wasted his life doing evil, robbing and killing. Then he waits until his dying hour to turn to God for mercy. He made a death-bed confession and now he expects to go to heaven. We want to say, "He doesn't deserve it. He should die for taking other people's property and lives. This man is on

15

the brink of hell and Jesus snatches him from the jaws of death. But, that is the way of Jesus. That is why we say his word is one of grace, love for condemned sinners. From the world's viewpoint it just does not make sense.

Paradise

Let us ask some questions about this word of grace, a promise. What was Jesus' promise? It was nothing less than heaven or paradise. To be in paradise is to have eternal life.

But what is the nature of paradise? When we know what it is, we may not want the promise for ourselves. Jesus describes and defines paradise in the words, "with me." "Today you will be with me in paradise." The best thing you can say about heaven is that it is a place where Jesus is. It is the greatest good and the best reason for wanting to go there. Paradise is more than a reunion with loved ones, as good as that may be. It is more than receiving rewards for faithful service to Christ. The only reward true Christians want is to be with Christ. Ignatius Loyola prayed: "Teach us, good Lord, to serve you as you deserve, to give and not to count the cost; to fight and not heed the wounds, to toil and not seek for rest; to labor and not to ask for any reward save that of knowing that we do your will."

The best thing about paradise is to be with the one you love the best. Jesus promises to be with us, to give himself to us. The only son of a Scotswoman became very successful in business. He provided for his mother by putting her in a comfortable house and showered her with gifts of money, clothes and jewelry. Yet, she was very unhappy. Her son noticed this and one day he asked her why she was so sad when he gave her everything she needed. She explained, "You give me everything but you have ceased to love me. You give me a home but you never stay in it to keep me company. You give me food but you do not eat with me. You give me everything but yourself." Paradise is heaven because Christ gives himself to us in order to be with us.

If paradise is being with Jesus, do we want to go there? If we do not care to be with Jesus here on earth, heaven will be hell for us. Do we honestly say, "I was glad when they said to me, 'Let us go into the house of the Lord'? " Can we say with Paul, "For me to live is Christ and to die is gain?" It is gain because to die means to be with Christ in paradise.

Today

We are given the promise of paradise, but when will the promise be fulfilled? Jesus said, "Today you will be with me in paradise." Heaven is for the here and now — "today." It is immediate. It begins when we accept Christ as our Lord and Savior. To be in Christ is to be in paradise.

There is no waiting for the promise to be fulfilled. A few years ago we visited an old cathedral in Toledo, Spain. In the floor close to a side altar was the grave of a cardinal. Over his grave a cardinal's hat was attached to the ceiling. According to legend when the hat fell, the soul of the cardinal would enter heaven. The hat has been hanging there for 400 years! If it takes 400 or more years for a cardinal to make it to heaven, how long would it take a common sinner to get there? Well, there is good news from Jesus: you can enter paradise today.

Therefore, we do not have to wait until death to go to paradise. According to the Bible, there is no Purgatory to delay our getting to heaven. Moreover, we do not have to wait for the resurrection of the dead at the end of time. Nor do we have to wait for the final judgment when Jesus returns to judge the nations, for Christians are judged here and now. Consequently, Christians do not face a final judgment because they are already in paradise with Christ. Our judgment is, when confronted with Christ, how we answer the question, "What then shall I do with Jesus?"

If heaven begins now, it is appropriate to ask, "Are you living in heaven right now? Are you a person in Christ? Are

17

you enjoying the love, peace and joy that come with being with Jesus? If not, why not?''

Remember

The gracious promise is paradise here and now. But who gets the promise? Everyone? There were two thieves on crosses, but only one got the promise. Indeed, Jesus would have promised paradise to both criminals, but one was not interested in being with Jesus and going to paradise. It is one thing to get a promise; it is another to claim it for oneself.

The one thief claimed the promise. He shows us how we, too, may claim it. A promise is the result of grace; the human response is faith. The thief, for one thing, made a request. He said, "Remember me when you come in your kingly power." This man wanted life after death, life with Jesus. With his whole heart he desired to live in paradise. For him life on earth was hell. If we would claim the promise, we, too, must want to be with Jesus in heaven more than anything else. "Ask and it will be given you."

The man got the promise because he also repented. This was shown by his confession of sin and that he deserved death. Before we can come to Jesus and be with him in paradise, we must truly repent of our sin. In recent years we hear very little about repentance. We would rather celebrate even when we do not know what we are celebrating! We are being told that to receive holy communion all we need is to be baptized. Yes, holy communion is for the people of God who have been baptized, but in addition we must be repentant, baptized people who are sorry for their sins and are determined to live a better life by the power of the Holy Spirit.

Add to this the requirement of faith to receive the promise. The repentant thief had that. By faith he knew Jesus was innocent and he told his fellow-criminal, "This man has done nothing wrong." He had the faith that enabled him to see that Jesus was a king and had kingly power. He saw by faith that he was more than a human. By faith, he entrusted the care of his soul into the hands of Jesus.

There is something tragic about this story of the three crosses. Here were two men with two eternal destinies. One went to heaven and the other to hell. One was saved and the other was lost. The tragedy is that both could have gone to paradise. Which of the two represents you? The famous astronomer, Copernicus, directed that this epitaph should be placed on his gravestone: "O Lord, the faith thou didst give to Paul, I cannot ask; the mercy thou didst show to Peter, I dare not ask; but, Lord, the grace thou didst show unto the dying robber, that, Lord, show to me."

A Grace Word Of Concern

The Third Word

Woman, here is your son! Here is your mother!
— John 19:26, 27

A prospective candidate for the priesthood had an interview with a priest in charge of admission at a Catholic seminary. The priest told his secretary not to put through any telephone calls unless it was from the archbishop or the pope. In the middle of the interview the phone rang. Though annoyed, he answered it. He was heard saying, "Yes, I told her not to let any calls through unless they came from the archbishop, the pope, or you — Mom!"

Who could refuse a mother's call? Is there anyone more important than a mother? Even when dying on the cross, Jesus could not ignore his mother. There she stood weeping at the foot of the cross. He must comfort and care for her. His heart went out to his broken-hearted mother. He has a word for her, a gracious word of concern.

21

Again, we see this word, "Here is your son," and "Here is your mother," as one of pure grace. The word seems so unnecessary and unreasonable. Why in his condition should he have to care for his mother? He had four brothers and more than one sister. Where were they? Why weren't they with their mother to care for and comfort her at this crisis in her life? It was their familial responsibility to care for her. In his love, Jesus establishes a new relationship between mother and son. He provides his mother a replacement son and gives John another mother.

A New Relationship Of Mother And Son

There is a common saying, "Blood is thicker than water." In the light of this new relationship established by the dying Jesus, it can be said, "Love is thicker than blood." It is not a blood but a love relationship.

From this third word from the cross, we see a new relationship between mother and son. He indicates that the old relationship has ended. He does not address her as "mother" but as "woman." Their relationship heretofore was a physical one, but now it must be spiritual. It was a human-to-human arrangement, but now it is human and divine. The physical had to decrease and the spiritual had to increase. By no means was this a disparagement or insult to his mother. It was telling it as it was and had to be. Now Mary had to see her son not as "my boy" but as her Lord and Savior. This man was more than a man; he was God's Son, "very God of very God, begotten not made, being of one substance with the Father" as we say in the Nicene creed.

This must have been a traumatic experience for Mary. For some time Jesus tried to prepare her for it. When he was 12, he asked, "Why did you seek me? Do you not know I must be in my Father's house?" At Cana when Mary told her son that the wedding party ran out of wine, he said, "O woman, what have you to do with me?"

22

This new relationship was good for Mother Mary. As a human, she was a sinner like all of us. She needed a Savior, a Mediator and an Advocate. Upon her son she would have to depend to make things right with God and gain her entrance into heaven.

It is good for us also. We need to be reminded who Jesus is. We have a tendency to see him as a human only. He is more than a friend, a big brother, a man for others. Jesus is the very Son of God, the Holy One. In contrast to us he is the sinless one. By his sacrifice on the cross, he opened the way to God's acceptance. We admire, respect, revere and adore him as "my Lord and my God."

A New Relationship Of People

While on the cross, Jesus created a new relationship between Mary and John. They were now mother and son. This relationship, of course, was not based on blood but on love.

People not physically related to each other can be closer and dearer to each other than spouses and children to each other. Consider the beautiful relationship between David and Jonathon, Saul's son. They confided in each other, protected each other, and were willing to die for each other. In like manner but with a change of sex, think of two women, Ruth and Naomi, a mother-in-law and a daughter-in-law. One of the most beautiful passages in the Bible consists of Ruth's "Entreat me not to leave you or to return from following you . . ." This is a classic example of the love and loyalty between two women.

Let me tell you about my own experience that illustrates the point. I have one brother who is totally different from me. He is heavily built and strong and I am on the light side. He has black hair and I have red hair. He is an extrovert and I am the opposite. He likes to party and I like to study. He is a dairyman and I am a preacher. He lives in the North and I live in the South. We have little if anything in common.

23

No one would guess that we are brothers. On the other hand, I have a friend with whom I roomed in seminary. For 55 years we have been the closest of friends: helping each other, corresponding, and getting together at summer school, conventions and vacations. It is a relationship not based on blood but on brotherly love.

This love relationship can be seen when a child is adopted. This adopted one can be as close and dear as a naturally born child. Recently we had a teaching-preaching mission in a church where the pastor and his wife had two children of their own, a girl and a boy who at age nine died of leukemia. Shortly after his death they adopted a baby girl who is now a teenager. You would never know she was adopted because of the close, loving relationship between her and the rest of the family. One does not have to be physically born of a couple to be a dear child.

A New Relationship With God

One day Jesus was preaching to a crowd. In the distance were his mother and brothers who wanted Jesus to come home with them. Some close to Jesus reported to him that his mother and brothers wanted him. In response Jesus asked, "Who are my mother and brothers?" He answered his own question: "Whoever does the will of God is my brother and sister and mother."

This opened up God's family to all who believed and obeyed God. This is what Jesus did, and all others who did the same became his family. Now there was a new relationship, not one of blood but of faith and obedience. If we have faith in Christ and "try his works to do," we are Jesus' mother, brothers and sisters.

At baptism a father-child relationship is established. By grace alone God forgives our sin and adopts us as his children. Consequently, we are the people of God, the family of God, the children of God. As such, we Christians become mothers, fathers, brothers and sisters in that family. We therefore could address each other as Mother Jane or Brother John or Sister Susie. If we are brothers and sisters, then how can it be that we in church are so cold, distant and unfriendly toward those we do not know intimately? If we are brothers and sisters in God's family, should we not care for each other as Jesus cared for his mother? Should we not send food to our brothers and sisters who are starving? Have we enough love for our Christian family to help them get out of an inner city ghetto where they are victims of drugs, poverty and crime? Many of our brothers and sisters are in trouble and need. Should we not out of love help them?

When we visited St. Peter's cathedral in Rome, we saw many wonderful works of art: paintings, statuary and frescoes. What impressed us most was Michelangelo's pure white marble statue, the Pieta, showing Mary holding in her lap her crucified son. She, at the time, is alive with deep sorrow and love shown on her face, and her son is dead. Soon, however, he will live again and she will die. Soon we, too, may die but we shall live because God's Son died for our sins.

A Grace Word Of Fidelity

The Fourth Word

My God, my God, why have you forsaken me?
                                    — Matthew 27:46

In a church in Gruyere, Switzerland, there is a large painting over the altar showing Jesus on the cross in all of his suffering. Upon a closer look one sees in the background God the Father who, reaching from heaven, upholds the cross with his two arms. It seems to say that God was at the crucifixion supporting and upholding his Son.

Does this painting contradict what Jesus cried with a loud voice, "My God, why have you forsaken me?" It was the lowest point in Jesus' life. He was on the cross now for three hours and death was near. Darkness covered the earth. Out of this dark night of the soul Jesus gave a piercing cry. It was so terrible that Matthew and Mark gave this as the only word spoken from the cross. It was a cry they could never forget, because they remembered Jesus' original words in his native tongue, Aramaic, "Eloi, Eloi, lama sabachthani."

27

It was not only a horrible cry of a dying man but also a troublesome thought. Did God really forsake his Son when he was needed the most? To say that God forsook Jesus is to bring into question the nature of God. Is he the kind of God who lets us down in a crisis? Moreover, the question is disturbing because if God forsook his Son, what makes us think that he would not desert plain, ordinary sinners like us? What do you think? Is the altar painting in the Swiss church correct that God was faithful to Jesus or was Jesus really forsaken by his Father?

Why Did He Say It?

If God the Father did not forsake his Son on the cross, why would Jesus say he was forsaken? Was he mistaken? Of course, Jesus never lied. Though Scripture does not give an answer, there are some possible answers to our question.

Jesus may have said he was forsaken because all his life he was acquainted with forsakenness. People constantly forsook him; why not God also? When he was born, there was no room in the inn and he had to be born with animals in a barn. "He came unto his own, and his own received him not." Before he was two years old, he had to flee to a foreign country to keep from being murdered by Herod. His first sermon at Nazareth was so poorly received that the people nearly threw him over a cliff to his death. His words and deeds were so upsetting to his immediate family that they considered him to be out of his mind. On Palm Sunday he offered himself to the nation as king of love, but he was rejected. With tears he moaned, "O Jerusalem, Jerusalem, how I would have gathered you, but you would not." When he was arrested and taken prisoner, his disciples forsook him and fled. One of the 12 betrayed him; another swore that he never knew him. Except for a few women and one man, he hangs on the cross — deserted and forsaken by all. And now God, too? Why not, everyone else did!

28

Maybe it was because of his sin, that he could not see God close at hand. No, it was not his sin because he never disobeyed God in any way. It was humanity's sin that was on his shoulders, like Atlas with the world on his, too. Paul tells us that Jesus became sin for us. To identify with humanity, he had to become a sinner so that he could pay the price for the sin of all people, past, present and future. Because of this sin, there came a feeling of forsakenness. Sin separates us from God. When Adam and Eve sinned, they fell away from God, from innocence to sin. This sin prohibits our seeing God, for sin blinds: "They know not what they are doing." God the Father was on Mount Calvary with Jesus — sharing the pain and pathos of his death. But, sin did not allow Jesus to realize his presence.

It may have been, further, that Jesus said he was forsaken because his suffering, pain and agony caused him to doubt and become negative in his feelings. We know from our own experience that when we have trouble, when we are in pain, when worry and fear plague us, we begin to question God's love and presence. Doubts assail us. We may become cynical and see good in nothing nor anyone. This is a feeling that comes over us in times of stress and misfortune. At times like the cross, it is not the absence of God but the absence of our experience of God. God is real and is present with us, but our condition does not allow us to have the experience of his presence. No doubt, this happened to Jesus, for no one ever suffered like he did on the cross, not only physically for two others that day endured the same physical torture, but also mentally and spiritually. At the time he felt he was forsaken, but, as feelings go, it was short-lived. In a little time, his Father was near, for he said, "Father, into your hands I commend my spirit."

A God Who Never Forsakes

We are not saying that Jesus was wrong when he asked why God had forsaken him. We are only saying that Jesus had a temporary feeling of being deserted, but soon his relationship was so close that in trust he turned his soul over to his Father who was with him all the time.

With complete confidence we can say, "God never, never forsakes anyone, especially not his Son. We hold to that because of God's nature which cannot change. The Bible says simply, "God is love." That is his nature. At one time God said, "I have loved you with an everlasting love." In 1 Corinthians 13 Paul says that love never fails and endures all things. True love never gives up and never deserts a loved one. In Romans 8 Paul asks, "Who shall separate us from the love of God?" It draws them to each other. It was love that made Ruth faithful to Naomi: "Your God shall be my God, where you die I will die." It is when love diminishes to nothing that friends become enemies and spouses separate. Where there is no love, there is no living together. For God to forsake Jesus would mean that God no longer loved his Son. That is impossible, for God's nature cannot change.

That takes us to another reason why we believe God did not forsake Jesus. It is the nature of God not to change. "From everlasting to everlasting thou art God." Jesus is like God: the same yesterday, today and forever. If God is love and that love accompanies and cares for us, then he cannot forsake his children. Repeatedly the refrain is heard, "His mercy endureth forever." The emphasis is on "forever," under all circumstances, any time of the year. Isn't this wonderful good news? God never ceases to love, care, help and bless us even when we deserve to be put on a cross for our wickedness.

Then, too, God never forsook Jesus and will never forsake us because God always keeps his promises. God's Word can be trusted. Never has he broken a promise. Look through the Bible and you will see God has never let one person down. When the three Hebrews were thrown into the fiery furnace, they were unharmed because there was a fourth man with them. God said he would be with us always, even in a fiery furnace of oppression. Remember these words of God: "I will never leave you nor forsake you." Did God break that promise on

Good Friday? God could not go back on his Word. That is not like God. He could not go against his nature of integrity. In the 23rd Psalm, we are assured that when we walk through the valley of death, "thou art with me." God is as good as his Word.

It is good to know, isn't it, that God did not forsake Jesus on the cross? It keeps our faith in a God whose love will never let us go and assures us that in our darkest hour he will be with us. So, once again we look at the altar painting in the Swiss church to see God's loving arms uplifting his beloved Son while dying for our sakes on the cross.

A Grace Word Of Need

The Fifth Word

I am thirsty.

— John 19:28

A man went into a jewelry store. He found a young lady to wait on him. He explained that he wanted to buy a cross. She asked, "Do you want a plain one or one with the little man on it?"

In this fifth Word from the cross, "I am thirsty," we have a cross with a man·on it. Indeed, he is 100 percent man as well as God. His humanity is as important as his divinity. This man, Jesus, is so human that he calls for a drink. It is so essential for a human to have water that a person can live only two days without water.

You may wonder, where is grace in this word from the cross? We think of grace in terms of giving, but grace is also receiving. In this case Jesus reveals grace by receiving a drink. Yes, where is grace in this cry for help: "I am thirsty?"

The Grace Of Humanity

Jesus' acknowledgment of thirst proves and reveals his humanity. Sometimes we forget that he is a human being. When we reflect on his teachings, we sense a divine wisdom. When we look at his flawless character, we know only God could be perfect like him. When we stand in awe at his miracles, we see the power of God in action. Though he is 100 percent God, he is also 100 percent man, and this fifth word from the cross reminds us of this fact.

It is grace that God became human in Jesus. As a human we see that we have a God who feels and hurts all of us. He is not a God like Buddha. Have you not seen a statue of Buddha sitting with feet under him, composed, serene, without any expression of joy or sorrow? Buddha is impervious to the world and people. Jesus is not so. He effects and affects the world. If Jesus did not call for help on the cross, he would not have been human. If he never said "ouch" when he was beaten, crowned with thorns, and had nails driven in hands and feet, he surely would have been only divine. With the heat beating on him, with the weight of his body tearing his flesh, with the flies gathered where he bled, with the malicious insults of the crowd, no wonder a human would respond with need.

"I am thirsty," reminds us that this Jesus on the cross was so human that he felt everything a human can feel. He could cry and laugh, struggle with temptation to disobey God; he could be tired and sleepy, hungry and thirsty. It is easy to imagine how he must have winced with pain when he was flogged and when those nails were hammered into his limbs.

What does his humanity mean to us today? It means that he is one of us. He shares our humanity with all its problems, joys and sorrows. He had his struggle with evil and was tempted like we are in every way. Because he shared in every facet of human life, he knows what we are going through. He was maligned by bigoted enemies as we may be. When we experience injustice in our courts, he also went through a mock trial. When we are mistreated and misunderstood, Jesus also was so badly treated that it made him weep. He knows our frame and what we are enduring. He has been there. He understands. By the grace of God and strength from God, he came out on top. His example assures us it can be the same with us if we put our trust in God.

The Grace Of Need

On the cross Jesus expressed he had a need. He was so very thirsty; his throat was parched. He needed a drink in the worst way. He said, "I am thirsty." He was unashamed to admit his need. It showed how human he was.

It is sometimes difficult for us to admit we are in need. We may be too proud to own up to it. To admit need indicates we are not self-sufficient, that we are dependent on others. We do not want to be indebted to others and feel obligated to return the favor. We pride ourselves in our independence and self-reliance.

As a result, some of us have a problem of receiving help or gifts from others. We want to be always on the giving end. This is much better for us. We are usually thanked. We make friends by what we give, and people express admiration and appreciation. But, how wrong we are by not wanting to receive from others! We deprive them of the joy and satisfaction of giving. By accepting their gifts or help we are encouraging their selflessness. A very poor but devout church member sent in her tithe. One day her pastor told her she need not give it, because she needed the money more than the church did. She replied, "Would you deny me the joy of giving to my Lord's work?"

We see in this fifth word not only the grace of need but of being needed. Jesus had the need; the soldier at the cross was needed to lift a sponge soaked with vinegar to Jesus' mouth for a drink. Don't you wish you could have been the one to give him the drink? What a privilege it would have been! Just as this soldier was needed, every one of us needs to be needed by someone. If nobody needs us, we feel useless and unnecessary in life. To be needed gives us a sense of purpose and reason for living. Because we are needed, we feel important. Otherwise, what is the sense of living? Nobody needs us.

An old street man became very ill. Police picked him up and took him to a hospital. Doctors realized he would not live long. They tried to get his name from him, but all he would say was "Son, Son!" Nurses looked in his clothes for identification but found none. All they found was a clipping of a marine stationed in Korea. The Red Cross contacted the marine and sent him back to the states and the hospital. When the marine walked into the room, the old man reached out his hand and said, "Son!" For hours the marine held his hand until he died. Then a nurse asked him for the name of his father. "He wasn't my father," explained the marine, "I never saw the man in my life." Startled, the nurse asked, "Then why did you stay?" He simply answered, "Because he needed me."

Yes, Christ needs us today as much as he needed someone to give him a drink. He needs each of us to tell the story of his love so that people will come to him and be saved. Otherwise, his sacrifice on the cross would be in vain.

Yes, he needs us to minister to the needs of the world. There are hungry, needy, thirsty, poor, sick and deprived people who need help. Jesus would minister to them all, but to do it, he needs us. When we feed the hungry, clothe the naked and visit the sick, he said we would be doing it for him and to him.

Christ needs us, and we need him even more than he needs us. Like Peter sinking into the Sea of Galilee while trying to walk on water, we cry out, "Lord, save me!" That is why we sing, "I need thee, precious Jesus. I need a friend like thee, a friend to soothe and pity, a friend to care for me."

As a human, Jesus thirsted for water and he received it — thanks to a kind Roman soldier. As the Son of God, he

thirsts for the souls of humanity — will he get them? As he
thirsts for us, may we also thirst for him: "As the heart panteth after the water brooks, so panteth my soul after thee, O
God."

A Grace Word Of Completion

The Sixth Word

It is finished.

— *John 19:30*

A few years ago Robert Burchfield completed the editing of the *Oxford English Dictionary* consisting of 13 volumes and 414,825 words. When he finished, he was asked which of the 414,825 words was his favorite. With a smile he declared, "Finished."

This word must also have been Jesus' favorite word on the cross, for on the cross he announced, "It is finished." It was a word of victory, joy and satisfaction that he completed the mission his Father gave him. To some extent I can understand his joy and satisfaction that he finished his work, because when I work day after day, week after week for a year reading, researching, reflecting, writing and re-writing a book, I feel like a load has been taken off my back when the book is finished and I sing, "Praise God from whom all blessings flow." Of the seven words of the cross, this word is the only one that gave Jesus some joy and satisfaction of a terrific job completed. It was a word of grace and a work of grace was finished.

What Was Finished

Surely Jesus could be glad that his torture was about over. His enemies' insults were over. He was finished with arguments with religious leaders. But something far more important was finished. His task of revealing the Father and his will was finished. When he died, the six-inch thick veil separating the holy of holies in the temple from the holy place was split in two. Now the nature of God could be seen. Jesus finished the task of revealing the truth of God. He is like Jesus, a God of love. "He who has seen me has seen the Father," he said. This love was described and demonstrated on the cross. A hymn has us sing:

> O dearly, dearly has he loved,
> And we must love him, too,
> And trust in his redeeming blood,
> And try his works to do.

Also, Jesus finished the work of revealing his own identity. Now we know that he was the long-promised Messiah, God's own Son. He lived as God wants us all to live. He showed us what it means to be a child of God. Now in Jesus we see that God wills for us to have character like Jesus and to give our lives in service to him and our neighbor. Through his teaching, miracles and especially in his suffering and death we can see that this strange man on the cross was none other than the Christ.

This means that we need not look for more or greater truth about God than Jesus gave to us. He is the perfect revelation of God. If we have the Bible, we need no other books that pretend to proclaim truth beyond the revelation of Christ.

40

There is no further truth in books such as *The Book of Mormon, Science and Health* and *The Divine Principle.* Even the church's tradition which teaches doctrines such as the Immaculate Conception, the Blessed Assumption, Purgatory and Papal Infallibility, does not exceed the truth revealed by Christ. All we need to know about God we see in Christ, and that revelation is found in the Bible.

Yes, his work of revelation was finished. Also, his work of redemption. Jesus was sent to the world to bring humanity back to God. It was God's plan of salvation to send Jesus as a human to die for humanity's sin. He did all that God demands of a human: perfect obedience to the law of God. He paid the price of humanity's disobedience by suffering and dying in mankind's place. As a result of Jesus' sacrifice, God is reconciled, pleased and satisfied. Jesus made things right between God and people, and brought both to an at-one-ment. What a terrific job that was! No other was good enough to do it. The task of redemption was finished. Now the gates of heaven were open to repentant sinners.

What does this completed work of redemption mean to us today? Now we know that there is no need to get right with God by our own efforts. The work has been done for us. Prayers, gifts and good works are of no use in getting God's favor. We cannot get to heaven by anything we say, do, or give. We are saved by grace alone through faith alone. By faith we accept Christ as our Savior upon whom we depend to set us right with God. With Augustus Toplady we sing:

Not the labors of my hands
Can fulfill thy law's demands;
Could my zeal no respite know,
Could my tears forever flow,
All for sin could not atone;
Thou must save, and Thou alone.

Are We Finished?

It is not how we begin but how we end our lives that counts. Many great people have had humble and poor beginnings but they had illustrious endings. Remember that Jesus was born in the poorest of conditions: in a barn with animals, from peasant parents and with despised shepherds as admirers. But, look how he finished; the cross turned out to be his glory!

Israel's first king, Saul, began as a promising young man, but he ended his reign hating David and committing suicide. Solomon was the wisest, richest and most powerful king in his day, but he ended up with God's displeasure because he turned to the false gods of his 1,000 wives and concubines. Judas Iscariot began as a disciple of promise, but ended up disowning his Master and killing himself. Richard Nixon in our generation held the highest office in the most powerful nation in the world but he ended up resigning as president because of unethical conduct. Pete Rose of baseball fame was at one time the best hitter, but he was dismissed in shame for his gambling. It is not how we begin life but whether we get to the finish line. It is good to make a great start, but faithfulness is required to end right. It calls for faithfulness to the task like the Roman soldier whose bones were found at the door where he stood on guard even when Vesuvius spewed forth lava and destroyed Pompeii. Someone forgot to relieve him from his duty.

When is a Christian finished with his work for God? Christ continued his work until the job was finished even at the cost of his life. Do we get tired of God and quit serving him? When we transfer our membership to a church in another location, do we refuse to move our membership to avoid getting involved? Even if we do transfer, do we just attend services and refuse to get involved in the program of the church? Is it not true that there is no retirement in God's business? There is no discharge in God's army. We are enlisted until we die as Christ finished by death on the cross. We cannot quit until "every knee shall bow and every tongue confess that Jesus Christ is Lord."

Of the 414,825 words in the dictionary, is "finished" your favorite word? No doubt, it was for Jesus, for it marked a victory for him over sin, Satan and death. It can be your favorite word, too, when at the end of life you can say with Paul: "I have fought a good fight, I have finished my course, I have kept the faith."

Let us pray: "O Lord, support us all day long of this troublous life, until the shadows lengthen, and the evening comes and the busy world is hushed, the fever of life is over and our work is done. Then, Lord, in thy mercy, grant us safe lodging, a holy rest and peace at the last; through Jesus Christ our Lord. Amen."

A Grace Word Of Commitment

The Seventh Word

Father, into your hands I commend my spirit.
— Luke 23:46

During World War II a United States regiment was about to leave for the invasion of France, across the English Channel. Before they went, they were given a concert in a theatre by those who wished them well. At the close of the concert the captain, in behalf of his troops, thanked them for their kindness and then with a broken voice he asked, "Ladies and Gentlemen, is there somebody here who can tell us how to die."

Since every one of us sooner or later is going to die, we, too, need someone to tell us how to die. Although 5,000 Americans die daily, some of us are not interested in learning how to die. Thinking death is far off in the future, young people don't want to consider it now. Yet, even young people die. In 1990 the top college basketball player, Hank Gathers, died at age 23 when he collapsed while playing a tournament game.

Older people also tend to dodge the fact of death. When someone speaks of dying, the response is, "Oh, don't talk like that!" Or, when we refer to the possibility of death, we avoid the word, death, by saying, "If something should happen to me." In Clearwater, Florida, a huge retirement complex with over 5,000 people has a monthly newsletter but obituaries are never printed. They want it, "Top of the World," to be a happy place to live.

It is as important to know how to die as it is to know how to live. In the hymn, "Go To Dark Gethsemane," we "Learn From Jesus Christ To Die." This seventh word from the cross teaches us how Jesus died. With complete trust in God, he prayed, "Father, into your hands I commend my spirit." It was a word of grace which enabled him to leave this life without fear or distress. With full confidence, he played his soul in the able, tender and everlasting hands of his Father.

Die In Christ

Most of us need to learn how to die with courage and in peace, for we are scared at the thought of death. It is the fear of the unknown. We do not know what will happen to us or where we will be. Just suppose a physician told us we had at most six months to live. Death is confronting us as Jesus confronted death on the cross. As Jesus lived the perfect life, he died the perfect death. Let us go to the cross and learn from him how to die.

To die like Christ, I need to die in Christ. If I am in Christ now by faith, I will be with Christ when earthly life is over. If he lives, so shall I. He said, "He that lives and believes in me shall never die." This does not mean we shall never die physically, but never spiritually. He is my Redeemer, Meditator, Advocate and Savior. By his sacrificial death, he has made things right with God for me. Because of Christ, God the Father forgives and accepts me as his child.

46

It is necessary, therefore, for me to live in Christ now, and someday to die in Christ. This means we need to always live in a state of grace so that it will not matter when death comes. When death approaches, faithful Christians desire to receive the Holy Communion, for through the broken body and shed blood of Christ we have a mystical union with Christ. The sacrament gives us assurance of God's forgiveness and our relationship with Christ is renewed.

Die In Faith

To learn to die is to learn to have faith in God and his Word. Faith replaces fear. We know so little about death and the hereafter that the only certain thing we have is God's Word. This calls for having faith in the Word and trust in God. With perfect trust, Jesus placed his spirit into God's hands and then died. You and I can do the same because of the goodness of God. He is a God who loves us and cares for us. He cared enough for sinners like you and me to die for us on the cross.

Not only do we need to have faith in the kind of God Jesus revealed, but we need to trust his Word with its promises. Jesus, the very Son of God, speaking for his Father, said, "In my father's house are many mansions . . . I go to prepare a place for you, that where I am you may be also." You and I have reservations in heaven, and at death we claim them. So then, I can die believing and trusting in God's Word. I know that he is a God who can be trusted. He has never failed to keep his promises and all of his promises have been fulfilled in Jesus. This enables me to relax in the face of death and fall asleep in God. William Cullen Bryant in "Thanatopsis" has these comforting words:

> So live, that when thy summons comes to join
> The innumerable caravan which moves
> To that mysterious realm, where each shall take
> His chamber in the silent halls of death,

47

Thou go not, like the quarry-slave at night,
Scourged to his dungeon, but sustained and soothed
By an unfaltering trust, approach thy grave
Like one that wraps the drapery of his couch
About him, and lies down in pleasant dreams.

Die In Hope

To learn to die is to die in hope. Jesus had hope that sustained him on the cross. He had the hope of the resurrection to which he frequently referred. He was looking forward to the day when he would return to heaven and have fellowship with his Father, the angels, and all the saints awaiting him.

We, too, can die in hope. We can see death not as an ending but as the beginning of life — more and better life than was possible on earth. As the sky is far above the earth, so life in heaven is far above in quality than life on earth. It is a place where all of our questions will be answered. All of our questions that ask, "Why, God?" will be answered to our satisfaction. It is a place where all our sorrows, troubles, doubts and fears will end. It is a place where we will see Jesus face to face and we will know him firsthand as he is. What a joy and privilege it will be to be in his presence! It is a place where we will have fellowship with our loved ones who died in Christ. There will be a great crowd of loved ones gathered to greet and welcome us when we arrive just as today friends come to the airport to meet our plane.

Death is a birth into a greater, finer life than anything we know on earth. It therefore is not something to be shunned nor feared, but welcomed. With joy we can anticipate death. Is that saying too much? Is that really true? Think of the glorious and beautiful things that await us. We have reason to hope for this experience. A little seven-year-old girl was dying from leukemia from which she had suffered for five years. Right before she died, she found enough strength to sit up and say, "The angels — they're so beautiful. Mommy, can you see

48

them? Do you hear them singing? I have never heard such beautiful singing!'' With the hope of having a like experience, we can die in hope as Jesus and this girl did.

We have been talking about our own death, but we must not forget that on the cross Someone died for us. One time a stranger rescued a small boy from drowning. After artificial respiration, he was brought back to consciousness and then looked into the face of the man who had saved him from a watery grave, and said, "Thank you, sir, for saving my life." The man replied, "That's all right, son; glad to do it. But see to it that you're worth saving." With that the stranger walked away, but the boy never forgot his words, "See to it that you're worth saving." Christ died to save you and me. Are we so living and serving that we are worth saving?

.